Born to Lose, Built to Win

Kerry Carter

DEDICATION

This book is dedicated to all the disbelievers who need to know that you can, and you should believe because your dreams can come true and will come true if you put in the work and push forward to achieve your dreams and your goals.

ACKNOWLEDGMENT

I'd like to knowledge Shannon. You've always put God first in life and let him lead the way, and Brandon Johnson, who has always been like a little brother to me. And Jonathan Simmons, for opening up my eyes that can help others do what he did for the blueprint has been laid.

CONTENTS

ABOUT THE AUTHOR

Born on 09.11.1970 in Houston, TX, I, Kerry Carter, lived in Houston for 43 years before I moved to California for five years. I worked under WES Crockett for three years under WesWorld Ent. where we signed some of the top fighters in the world who later went on to become World Champion boxers. From there on, I went on to become someone who helped athletes.

PREFACE

Our lives are very much dependent on what we have. While that is true, there lies another fact, and that is the clarity we often blind ourselves to. Our lives are also highly dependent on what we create with what we have. This, however, requires immense patience and faith. Faith can be in our own selves or in a higher power.

In times when nothing is available or bright, it can be tough to have faith or even maintain it. But the reality gets easier when we realize a secret: the world is ours to create. It is not our job to complete every job from start to finish. Our job is to do what we can within our reach. And then it is up to our Lord. We can only do as much as our capacity allows. When we try to reach out to that, we feel as if we are falling. Although we are not, our brain makes us think otherwise. The key is to focus on yourself, your goals, your strength and convert your weakness into your strength.

This is why faith is solid. This is why we lean on faith and ask for it to hold us when we fall weak. So that we don't fall onto the ground but onto it for support. Faith is wide, way beyond our reach. It is what holds us when we fall and what backs us up when we rise.

All faith requires from us is also faith. Faith in itself, faith in its wonders.

CHAPTER 1:
UNCERTAINTY

The only thing certain in life is uncertainty. We live our lives planning for a time when certainty will encircle us, and we'll breathe a deep sigh. We work to achieve success, but more than that, we work towards validation. We require validation from family, friends, and more so, from ourselves. What we sometimes forget is that the only support to lean on for such validation is God.

Faith in Him is what leads us to believe in ourselves because do we really have a choice? We will clutch onto love that is faithful, honest, and unconditional. Such love helps us walk through life because we have faith in the power that we know takes care of us. Your success depends heavily on what you make with what you have and the belief that you can make it through. After all, why can't you?

Failures have a way of making us question ourselves and our decisions, but it also does us a favor – it provides us clarity. We can be clear on who we are, what we want to achieve, and it is like the smell of the air after a storm passes through. Our failure is our biggest lesson because that is when our strength comes out.

Our strength needs to show up in the time of need, and it needs to take action and come at a time of help. In our most vulnerable state, we seek help, we seek to support, and most of all, we look for a shoulder to lean on to be our walking stick. When uncertainty walks through our main door, our eyes are rather alert and our eyes wide open. It is then that the decisions we take impact us. In an acute crisis or situation, while the decisions we take are based on what we are thinking at that point in time, they are also hugely based on the way we have handled situations in the past and how capable we are based on past experiences.

For me, life played a role that had me keeping my emotions in check all the time. I was always thrown into situations at the speed of lightning. The uncertainty came to me like a friend, like an enemy, like a confused kid, like a damaged adult, and most of all, like a human who survives on faith. For the most part, I survived life with a single mother. A woman made of steel, my mother made sure she was a force of strength, one to be reckoned with. Perhaps, that's where I received my strength from. My father had passed away, and so my mother was left with no choice but to take care of me all by herself.

Before your dream comes to life, the time when it is under construction, we have many questions. Some of those questions are within our reach and many beyond. We start off our lives full of dreams that soar in the sky. Unfortunately, the distance between the ground and the sky interrupts and makes us question our plans. However, we are so motivated that we don't feel bothered by it. Until one day, it gets to us. We know we can fly, so we spend time figuring out how to fly, and, in the process, we tend to get tired. With contributions from external sources and our own insecurities, we find ourselves struggling to crawl.

Every morning, we wake up with the goal to achieve. We wake up wanting to fulfill what we aspire to, and to a certain extent, we do. For example, in the kitchen, we realize we will not be served every ingredient we need to make the best dish. Instead, we will need to know the process best in order to get the cooking going. Similarly, we fall, we stumble, but we make it through. Perhaps, this may be because we know it's really the only choice we have. We polish ourselves and learn from our experiences so that they may help us when we do not have the space to think. The future is relentless, but it is also fierce. It allows you to be fierce and take your space when you need it and how you need it. But for that, it needs to prepare you too. And so it does, with the hardships it throws at you.

When we are on the mission to achieve something, we don't pay heed to what may harm us because we know the fire within us will save us. The uncertainty of a situation gives us confidence that we will achieve our goals because the result is uncertain, right? But there comes a time when it gets to us, and at that point, we don't know what to do. That is when we are stuck. I can say this because I have been there. When uncertainty catches up to you, what do you do?

Well, you move on. And you move on with your head held high. Uncertainty catches up to us the most when we are certain. It holds onto us and makes us feel invalid. My life took a certain turn as well. There came a time when the only one I had was my mother. She was my rock and the woman I learned strength from.

I remember the time when my mother was all I had and the only one I ever needed. Our lives were very uncertain, and the only certainty in my life was my mother. I remember running from pillow to post, not having a stable home. My mother and I were living on an hour-to-hour basis and trying to make it through the day. We would not save up for the next day because our purpose was to put food on the table for that night.

I vividly remember running attending three different elementary schools in one year because our lives were so unstable. I did think the uncertainty was detrimental, but we had no choice. We were trying to survive first. But that's not the worst. I remember being home with one of my mother's boyfriends at the time while she was at work and experiencing abuse. He used to abuse me physically by beating me vigorously, mercilessly. He would also burn me with cigarettes and use hot iron rods on my body and make attempts to hurt me with every chance he got. My mother did not know for the longest time because she was romantically involved with him. Regardless of his treatment, I pushed myself to be the best version of myself and strived to achieve my goals. This is because I knew I was the only one who could fix myself and that other people's opinions of me would not define who I am or where I stand in life. This energy and thought process helped me keep a hold of myself and establish myself as I was and where I stood.

You will be pushed and pulled. You will be thrown to the ground and pulled back up only to be thrown back again. But that does not mean that you let the bully have their way. It is then that you stand up and fight for yourself. The biggest lesson you can always learn is to stand up for who you are and what you believe in. You can be beaten down physically, emotionally, and mentally. People can take away your money, block your roads, and hinder your path, but they can never take away your faith. They cannot take away your purpose. They cannot take away your reason to be and the goals you aspire to achieve. I believed my faith would take me places, and it did. It was my rock because I realized our problems would not end, but our courage would increase in levels. God sends us through trials and tribulations to teach us lessons that will help us make decisions in the future and stabilize us for what's to come. Life will not come to us easily, and it will also not come with solutions. We will have to create solutions and extract answers from our questions.

As a child, you lean on your parents for support. Your mother and father provide you shelter, not just financially or physically, but also in terms of our existence. Our parents establish our foundation by teaching us values and helping us understand how to function in life and choose a route for ourselves. Since my father had passed away and my mother never told me who he was, I always leaned on my mother for support. I would not always get it from her, and so, I clutched onto faith. I would look up to the sky and think that my father was in heaven. I never said it out loud in the past, but over time, I came to realize that my mother was selfish and when I look back at certain occasions, it hits me; she really just thought about herself. Perhaps, that's why I came up with the title "Born to Lose, Built to Win." Because we are, we are born a certain way, but as we grow, we negate that theory and make one of our own. We create our own path with our own struggles and opinions. We build ourselves from ourselves.

Do you remember the times when we were young and dreamt of the times when we would grow up and become who we wanted to be? Some of us aspired to become a policeman or a fireman, while many of us dreamt of existing in space as an astronaut. Many wanted to be the ones who provided justice, and so we dreamt of becoming a lawyer. I remember those days as if they took place yesterday. This is because I'm aware that with the right encouragement and support, we can become all that we aspire to be.

Inside us exists a little bird that gives us an unbiased insight into reality. That little bird is not influenced by our heart or our mind; it does not prefer logic over emotions or emotions over logic. The little bird is rational and realistic. That little bird is our gut. Our gut feelings are almost never wrong – they're honest, raw, and subtle. It can be difficult to differentiate our gut feeling from what our heart and mind are saying, but if you truly focus, you'll know which is what.

That little bird is the one that tells us never to quit. The bird convinces us to push through regardless of the circumstances because humans are meant for greater achievements. This little bird is the voice that resides within us, and it pushes us to achieve more because it is not influenced by the negativity that influences our life. The little voice convinces us never to give up. The motivation to not give up is what gives us the strength we need to keep pushing forward and fight for our dreams. We exist less as who we are and more as who we could be.

We learn that life does not owe us an explanation because it's well-aware of what is lying down in front of us. Our strength needs to come from us, and it needs to divide within us. We cannot rely on anyone to provide us support because it will leave when that person leaves us. Faith, however, works differently. Faith allows us to feel because it gives us the space to grieve. Faith gives us the space to be ourselves and not feel dejected about it. It does not provide us unsolicited advice, and most importantly, it does not invalidate our pain.

Human beings will validate your pain to the extent it suits them. They will validate on their own terms with what they feel is correct and what they feel can be let go of. This is why one of our greatest learnings includes our growth. We owe it to ourselves to create success out of nothing but our talent, our vision, and our aspirations. We need to weave our basket of achievements and failures ourselves because only we can know how to interlace them altogether.

Throughout our life, we will encounter many obstacles that will continue to stand in our way adamantly. That can take a serious toll on our mental health and drain us physically. These obstacles diligently try to discourage us, time and time again. On the surface level, some of these issues may include lack of financial backing, poverty, drug addiction, self-esteem issues, health issues, domestic violence, abuse, family conflict, body image issues, racism, and a compromise on mental health. Such problems, amongst others, can heavily impact us and, more so, the decisions we may choose to make. We may jeopardize our dreams because of what our self-esteem is feeding us. This is where we need to be there for ourselves the most. We need to be present and consciously train our own minds of all that we are capable of.

When we are close to achieving our dreams, we often hold a debate against ourselves in an attempt to see whether we should give up or continue battling. Most of us may give up, but some of us may not. The battle changes its route based on the decision you make at this point, and that's where change begins. Your life will change when you accept that your comfort zone is not a place for you to grow.

In order to grow, you need to extract from your life what you think promotes giving up. Change starts small. Let's start from the basics. The language we use daily affects our mood, our willpower, and our perception. From personal experience, I can say: slowly eliminate the letter Q from your vocabulary. This letter is not meant for us. Q stands for Quit, which subsequently leads to the idea of giving up. Quitting may seem tempting, but its consequences are beyond the surface level. It is easier said than done, but stretching it far, brick by brick is a smart strategy as well. Jacob A. Riis said,

"When nothing seems to help, I go and look at a stonecutter hammering away at his rock, perhaps a hundred times without as much as a crack showing in it. Yet at the hundred and first blow it will split in two, and I know it was not that last blow that did it, but all that had gone before."

Your results will reap the rewards right when you want to give up because you have reached them thus far. When you reach the finish line, it is perhaps only you can relive your win as you sigh in relief. You look at how far you've come and the person you have evolved into. It is you who can decipher what would have happened had you quit. I can think of five situations where my encouragement helped play a significant part in the lives of five young men. I helped them push forward to become successful people who were an asset to the society they belonged to and a ray of hope regardless of where they went.

CHAPTER 2:
Shoot! Swing!

Later in life, I met two young boys who were prime examples of how far hard work can take you if you are honest throughout. The young men were twin brothers: Jamal and Jamel. The two boys were somewhat unique in terms of their drive and passion for succeeding. Jamal and Jamel were little boys, but they were thirsty to make it into the boxing world. They submitted their life to boxing and put in efforts beyond what is humanly possible to achieve success.

I had the pleasure of meeting Jamal and Jamel in 2011 in Houston, Texas. When I initially met them, they were youthful and putting in their blood and sweat to make it through somehow. I knew the twin brother had talent, but what I also learned was that they did not let any external factors hinder their success. This is why I wanted to help them- I wanted to be a part of their success. I vividly remember Jamal and Jamel entering the gym every day, training like they were unfailingly conquerors. The two twins went through difficult times because they were having trouble with how they were being managed. Their management became a grave concern soon enough with the shift in different managers consistently. One after the other, the boys hired and fired managers.

One of those days, they were having a rather stressful time, and I felt a pittish feeling in my stomach considering their situation.

The boys were rather hard-working, and seeing them struggle pulled my heartstrings apart. They needed help, and so I offered it. I took the boys under my wing and signed them to Wes World under the ownership of Big Wes. I utilized my contacts and led the twin brothers to a safe space. Both the brothers received a total of $35,000.00 signing bonus and a monthly pay of $3500. Jamal and Jamel were thrilled and even more motivated for what was to come. The two brothers knew it was the start of their journey and that they were on the way to signing with one of the world's most successful management companies: Al Haymon.

The twins knew signing with a reputable boxing manager was not served on a silver platter to anyone, but they were grateful. They took advantage of this situation and invested in all their energy towards making it big.

Six years later, Jamal and Jamel became world champions. The twin brothers were now capable of providing a life for their families, ones they were proud of. The boys formed their mother's heart and constructed their father's soul. The two boys were loved immensely by their parents, and this acted as their greatest motivation. I was incredibly proud of them. Never have any of the two disappointed me with regards to anything during the course of my engagement with them.

I believe God played a remarkable role in this entire process. While we see the bigger picture, God considers the more comprehensive picture. We may be denied one thing in life because something else fits us better. But then we stop to think,

"If God is that powerful, why did he not place his blessings in what I already had?"

Perhaps we will never receive answers for the questions we ask Him, but God has His ways. God's power resides in his actions and how he manages to place our life on track in a way that we don't realize. God is magnificent, and he is the kindest. When all else fails, and hopelessness encircles us, faith holds us tight. God places us in the lives of people so that we may help them. Helping others is an act that makes us feel better about ourselves. It gets easier to continue our mission and not quit after we place our faith in God.

I believe I was only a source of help for the twin brothers. It was their dedication and faith in God that helped them surpass their struggles and succeed.

Many times, we require the help of people to reach mountain tops. This does not mean that we are not competent or that we don't have the skills necessary to succeed. Getting to different places in life will require asking for help from people who can help us get there. There is no shame in asking for help, for humans were created for each other. All of us are meant to help someone or the other in ways we are yet to discover.

Your ego is not compromised, and your self-respect is not harmed if you ask for help. This is a chain that follows. When we succeed because someone has helped us, we find ourselves in a position to help other people. I did not have a childhood many children have. My mother worked day and night to make ends meet. I am now in a capable space to help those who are genuinely in need, and so I believe God has blessed me by allowing me to help other people.

When you are at your lowest, receiving support can help immensely, especially in terms of boosting self-esteem. When someone is present, physically and emotionally, it feels as if you're not alone because someone is holding your hand. You're not walking through the dark alley alone; you have a shadow overlooking you. That shadow is God. God has a way of being present for us in ways the human mind can not decipher. God makes himself present in our lives through the blessings he bestows upon us - his people. God sends us people who can help us get through our tough times so that we may become the best version of ourselves. That extra push can save us more than we anticipate; perhaps, it was the only push we really needed to take that jump.

The people in our life help us by making us feel important, trusted, loved, and validated. Perhaps, what everyone is seeking is validation. Validation is an affirmation. In a moment of weakness, receiving validation can significantly help in stabilizing an individual's morale. If that is not God's help, then what is?

In a world where everyone is replaceable, being left behind can make an individual feel as if they're next. All of us require someone to stand with us and make us feel as if we can trust them with our vulnerabilities. For it is our vulnerability that makes us human, that allows us to feel the pain of other people which then translates to wanting to help them.

Jamal and Jamel were filled with talent, purpose, and direction. What the boys required was someone who could lead them and help them reach their destination. Their success is a result of their ongoing hard work, resilience, patience, and, more importantly, the will to change their life.

As much as we are a source of help for many, a more excellent query is the acceptance of help. Why should an individual accept help? We sometimes may feel as if we're a burden on the people around us, which includes our family and our friends. We feel guilty of needing help; after all, should we achieve our mission independently? Why should we accept help from our family or friends? In more extreme cases, why should individuals receive help from outsiders? I, Kerry Carter, was a man utterly unknown to Jamal and Jamel, yet I helped them. And they accepted it. Providing help and getting help both have one element in common: *humans need humans.*

We need to learn to consider help as one of God's blessings and not as a compromise of our self-respect. We are all different pieces of the same puzzle, and it's a matter of which pieces fit together. We cannot fulfill our purpose single-handedly because we all have a role to play in each other's success. Maybe that's why success has a different taste to it – one of contentment.

CHAPTER 3:
DREAMS KNOW NO AGE

It is a well-known fact that when you invest your mind in a purpose, it reaps you rewards that continue to benefit you for years to come. Faith has more power than the human mind can ever calculate.

I knew Jamal and Jamel had endless potential. I was aware of how far they would go, but I could not anticipate that they would become world-class champions one day. I assumed they would become champions in different weight classes, but they outdid themselves. Faith is the thread that holds us when we feel like we're falling. It pulls us through tough times and more challenging moments.

I'm a firm believer in,

"So the mind think it,

so it shall be

So the tongue speak it,

it shall come to be."

The Bible talks about faith and what it can do for you. That's what I can vouch for regarding the twins. Jamal and Jamel believed in what they said, and it came to life, or should I say reality. When you view yourself in the mirror, you will notice it's the same person you saw yesterday and the week before, and the week before that. The only existing difference would be the difference in the number of days since you last saw yourself and now.

Our success begins walking to us when we realize that we are capable of achieving all that we aspire to, and it comes running to us when we embark on that journey regardless of the hurdles that may come our way. This is because as many hurdles as we may across, our resilience will always be greater than our obstacles. What you do today must prepare you for tomorrow, and tomorrow's goal should bring you one day closer to your dream. All of us aspire to become something special, but what are you doing to achieve that dream?

More importantly, the question remains: what will we do when we become something special? Are we ready to handle it? What will we do after we've become special? We may reach a dead-end, and more specifically, we may lose our sense of purpose. This is why a plan of action is crucial.

Dreams have no age; they can hit you at any point. However, when you fulfill one dream, another comes running. When you meet another dream, the third one may come flying. Your stability should not depend on your dreams, and your desires should.

Many people reject their chances to wait for the right time, but the question is,

How can you wait for the right time when you don't know what the future holds?

The future is as uncertain as it gets. It holds surprises, yet no accountability. Once we learn the pattern the system of life follows, we will understand that the ultimate control is in our own hands. Even if we are thrown obstacles that may hinder our plans or our growth, we are still the ones who take that final decision.

So, what defines time as right or wrong? How can an individual know that the time is right? and who settles these patterns? I'm here to tell you that the time is right when you have the ability to chase your dreams. I'm here also to tell you that you don't have to wait till the time is right.

The older you get, the more your chances of doing what you love will slim down. As we get older, we accumulate more responsibility. As responsibilities increase, debts increase. As we begin to age, we slowly put our dreams and aspirations in the backseat and place our responsibilities in the front seat. When we shift something to tomorrow, we fundamentally convince ourselves that it's not urgent and it can wait. Normally, that would mean prioritizing other matters at hand. However, if we dig deep down, it would mean the same thing, just more substantially concerning.

We don't have control over natural occurrences, for instance: death, illness, or calamity. So, if you are not facing a natural occurrence, you are in the perfect space to run after your dreams because you still have control. It is only after we lose our power that we realize the intensity of the energy we have.

In an attempt to pay off our debts, we place our lives on hold. Our dreams exit the equation, and our compulsions dive in. What this does is that it sets a track record. It forms an expectation we have from ourselves. Just as water seeps in through a damaged wall and the leakage gets out of control, our responsibilities get the best of us and convince us that our parents need us more, or our siblings need us more, or that life is not about our goals at this point.

When we begin to feed our responsibilities, we essentially prepare ourselves to never look after ourselves; or, in this case, our dreams. Before we realize it, we are a part of the 9 to 5 job culture, and our dreams of making it big are full of dust. They have not died; our dreams are very much alive. However, they have encapsulated themselves inside a hollow cave and shut out any possible entries. That cave does not disturb us, but it does consume space, and that wrecks us apart.

People will continue working 9 to 5 for twenty to thirty years until they look back and realize there's not much they have achieved for themselves. However, by the time they do figure it out, it's slightly too late. We don't realize this till the end, but the reality is indeed something else. The crux of the matter is that in order to recover from the hurt they have wrapped and kept aside, individuals convince themselves that their contentment lies in working for others. Thus, they fill the gaps of their heart by existing for other people.

I have heard this in the past, and I continue to hear it even now: people talk about their desire to start their own business. I, in turn, ask them, "why not?"

The difference between a boss and a subordinate is the fact that they took a chance on themselves and landed themselves a position that speaks for them. Your boss accepted your job proposal because they noticed the talent in you. They pay you dollars as you provide them labor. Your talent, energy, and intelligence are providing a rather lot of benefit to your boss – something that you have the potential to lead.

The energy you infuse in your job is the same energy that is required for you to work on something you can call your own. Your boss is paying you a check at the end of every month but what you are doing is beyond. You don't need to limit yourself to living paycheck-to-paycheck every month.

The real success is in learning that failing is not dangerous. It is not a problem if you fail or are close to failing. You don't need to panic, and you don't need to attack your self-worth for it. What I have noticed over the course of my career is that many people don't embark on a specific journey because of the fear of failure that clouds them. Perhaps, the most effective advice you can give yourself is that failure is a part of what you are, just like success is. Success cannot exist where failure is absent, and failure cannot feed a place that lacks the potential to succeed. The two go hand-in-hand, and perhaps, that's where the thrill lies: In not knowing, "what if you succeed?"

Another aspect that can pose as an issue is lesser-known but relatively common. It is the fear of success. Many worry about what they'll do if they fail. However, some fear the result of what may happen when they succeed.

The fear of success is more often known as success anxiety. With the fear of success, individuals are afraid of the result of success in their lives. They are conscious of a negative impact on their lifestyle and the idea of expecting more. An overwhelming fear of change can make us anxious and make us feel as if we'll lose what we have; our comfort zone. As human beings who are always planning the next move, or the next step, we feed off of routine and a map of where we are meant to be and how much it will stabilize us, either financially or mentally. With an expectation of success, many changes, and we're not sure of what will stay. This makes us feel lonely and questions if the success we achieve is worth it.

When we do adapt to change and lack knowing what the next step may be, we begin to expect. That can be more emotionally taxing rather than frightening. When we achieve something, we hope more, and then more, and then more. When those expectations are not met, we are demoralized. We expect more from the people around us, from our leads, from our job, and, more importantly, from ourselves. What we tend to forget in this entire process is that we are merely humans.

The reality is that you might succeed, and you might not. However, you cannot reach a conclusion until and unless you don't try.

As Erin Hanson says,

"What if I fail?

Oh, but my darling, what if you fly?"

Once we understand that failing is an inevitable part of life, we realize that any decision we base on the fear of failure is nullified. We realize we are simply wasting our time then because, as humans, we can't fight the inevitable. We are born to stand in the face of the inevitable and win despite the barriers they project on us.

You won't necessarily win; for instance: you're starting a new business and are taking a risk because you are unaware of how well it will or will not do. The fact remains that you will only ever receive your answers *if you try*. If you have not lived through something, how will you know what the result maybe? Now, the question here changes slightly:

"Is the risk worth it?"

Do you notice the difference? You've taken power away from the inevitable and placed it back in your hands. If you choose not to go forward with your start-up now, it will be because you don't find it rewarding enough. The decision was in your hands, and you made it. The power of decision-making plays a huge role in our growth and how we continue to view ourselves. In this case, your confidence will rise, and you will trust yourself more often because you have faith in your decision.

We may not know much about the world we live in or what the future holds, but we do know that we get one life. You get one life to do anything you want, in any way you want. You have no restrictions in terms of availability, and your potential to succeed is beyond. How do you choose to utilize it? Do you want to live a life of fear and reject even the slightest chance you have to succeed? Or are you content with the life you are currently living?

We spend so much time stressing over what could have been and, more importantly, what we want it to be, that we forget we are in the now. You don't know if you will live to see tomorrow, and so, thank the Lord for today. You never know, his generosity may exceed for you, and He may bless you with more than your accumulated gain that week.

The key here is to take full advantage of the opportunity He has blessed you with. Think about what God has blessed you with and how He can give so much more. If He granted you this much without you asking for it, it is only up to your imagination to think how He would bless you if you ask Him for all that you want. This is where the fear of failure also diminishes. Once you embark on a journey to achieve what you want, and you keep God with you at every step of the way, you will not fail. More importantly, you will not feel alone.

Faith in God is like a stabilizer. It will keep you solid in the now and hopeful for the future. He had created us, and he has blessed us all in different ways. Some of us are talented in some ways, while many of us are talented in other ways. By this phenomenon, everyone is talented and God-gifted. So, if your heart is inclined towards something, it is mainly because God has embedded that certain something within you. Then how can you fail?

If you have a great voice, it's a sign from God. You can hold external factors accountable, but you won't go much far. Believe me, someone exists. Someone who wishes they had a voice, someone who is in desperate need to talk. But they can't. When we compare our blessings with other people, we realize we were looking on the other side of the road all this time. Many are devoid of the opportunity to speak a word simply, but they can't. So, if you have a lovely voice, use it. Your talent is your biggest evidence. It is proof of who you are and how far you are bound to go in order to succeed.

I say this with personal experience and with the experience of seeing other people; we realize all that we had after we lose. Our dreams are timeless and limitless because they are dreams. It is us, humans, who place a deadline or boundary to it. When we understand that the essence of our dreams lies in their characteristic of being infinite, we truly begin to see the extent of our talent and skill. It starts when you accept that you are genuinely and magnificently blessed.

CHAPTER 4:
BRANDON JOHNSON

I have always believed in the power of faith. Faith is not simply a religion; it is the belief that you are being looked after and, more importantly, you are not alone. This helps in times of hopelessness and when fear looms over us. God places people in our lives for a purpose and also makes sure that we have played our role in their lives before matters escalate or take a turn.

One such example is of a young man named Brandon Johnson. Brandon went to the University of San Diego and was a man of reason. He was solid and directed. He knew what he wanted, and his passion was as strong as flames in a bonfire – it never died. God crossed my path with Brandon Johnson in 2010 at a basketball tournament I founded a year ago. I began that tournament in 209, and a year later, in 2010, I met Brandon. The tournament was called The Texas Shootout. I witnessed Brandon playing with a team called New Era. Brandon stood out like no other player I've ever seen besides the NBA experience. Brandon was solid in his game and played with honesty. More than anything, Brandon was authentic, and that showed in the game he played. A good basketball player does not win every game; he's someone who plays with their heart and has the thirst to be better at the next game.

Brandon's vision was impeccable. His strategy was not influenced by anyone, and he knew it was purely his hard work that mattered. He was well aware that only he could fix the messy aspects of the game, which included the late nights, the blood and sweat, and deceptive thoughts. Brandon would always say one thing and one thing only,

"No one can stop me, or should I say, no one can hold me inside the court."

Brandon succeeded because he believed in himself. He believed in who he could be, and he made it happen. That showed in his game. His energy, his demeanor all reflected his conviction and goal. He was a well-rounded player. When I asked other people about him, I would look for someone to convey insight, which doesn't come out in public but still exists. Anyone I spoke to told me the same thing: he's a pro. There was not a single negative remark regarding Brandon, and that was, perhaps, more than enough for me to know that he was going to be alright.

One day, after his game, I approached Brandon and took him to a side in an attempt to start a conversation.

"Hey Brandon, great game man. Congratulations." I said excitedly as I shook his hand.

"Thanks, man."

"How you feelin'?"

"I'm great, I'm great. Thank you. I'm sorry I don't know your name?"

"Oh! I'm Kerry. I hold basketball tournaments around the country. I actually wanted to ask you if you would want to travel to San Antonio with my team."

"Well, umm… I'm not sure if my team is going or not. How about I let you know?"

"Sure."

The tournament was supposed to take place the following weekend, and Brandon hadn't gotten back to me. I moved on and traveled to San Antonio for the tournament. As I pulled up to my gym in San Antonio, I found Brandon standing at the front gate of the building, waiting for me.

"Hey, so do you still want me around?"

"OF COURSE I DO, BOY!"

This is why my faith in nature and God is so deep-rooted. What is meant for you will always reach you. You will receive what you require to succeed, and if you don't get it, then there's something else that fits your puzzle better. Brandon then put on my Houston Live uniform, and he hasn't taken it off for seven years now. Brandon has become an essential part of Houston Live and is one of our most highly-regarded souls.

Now that you know God handpicked us and placed us in each other's lives, I'll move on to his testimony. Let me tell you more about how God utilized me to push Brandon to keep fighting for his dream. We are all always placed in people's lives, and there's always a reason. God placed me in his life so that I could help elevate him and make him realize his true potential.

At the University of San Diego, Brandon Johnson was a star player. He was used as an example for many. He led his team to the NCAA's Final Four Tournament in 2008, where the team played #4Connecticut. Brandon scored 16.9 Points, 4.1 Reb, and 3.5 Ast, beating #4 Connecticut 70-69. Brandon was considered to be one of the topmost recruits in the NBA draft that year.

However, an investigation was conducted due to reasons the authorities found questionable. After further investigation, it was discovered that Brandon was involved in what is known as Point Shaving. Point Shaving can be more simply defined as a type of match-fixing whereby perpetrators try to prevent a team from covering a published point spread. Unlike other forms of sports betting, spread betting invariably motivates. Point shaving is a type of match-fixing strategy that impacts the win because one or some members of the team consciously mess with the point spread. This is considered a crime in sports literature because you are not just winning illegally but also jeopardizing the other team.

Consequently, Brandon's basketball career reached a pitstop. Brandon could not play for a long while in the NBA, but the boy did not lose faith. Brandon could have complained about everything. He had the perfect opportunity to blame his circumstance, his position, God and ask for answers. He could have cried over losing all that he achieved, but he chose to be patient. What kept Brandon stable was his belief in his potential and faith in his honesty. The kid knew he was genuine in his game, and that's why his strength never died down. I learned quite a lot from Brandon and the way he perceived tough times.

Brandon was humble and pragmatic; his personality was that of someone who knew life would not serve desserts on a plate and that too, every day. When you have good days, you will also have bad days. His conviction was one to learn from.

Brandon believed in who he was, regardless of the allegations that were thrown at him. He never gave up on his dream of becoming a basketball player. I once asked him,

"Don't you feel demotivated?"

"About what, Kerry?"

"You have such strong allegations against you. How are you still so solid."

"Because I know myself. The public doesn't know the kind of person I am, but I also can't blame them for not knowing. They've only seen me play. But I'm honest with myself, and this is why I know I will succeed."

"Where do you retrieve this confidence from?"

"I know someone's looking after me, and that's God. Also, from the energy I infuse into my game. It helps me grow as a person. God won't fail me if I'm honest."

"I really do hope and pray you to succeed, my young child. You'll soar the sky."

"Thanks, chief."

Brandon's belief in God was unwavering. Over time, Brandon and I became brothers, whereby he trusted me just like he would trust an older brother. After the NBA closed its doors on him and after receiving a knee surgery that jeopardized his ability to play, God blessed us with His mercy. He showed that there is nothing impossible for Him; all we have to do is *ask*. God is willing to give us all we want; however, we need to ask Him to give it to us. God is the kindest because His love for us extends to the heavens and Earth. It is not conditional and limited, and Brandon knew that. Today, Brandon is earning six figures and playing basketball professionally overseas.

It is a rather cliché statement, but if Brandon can make it work, so can you.

This is a tough but very important reality that many of us run away from. Only we can help ourselves. We can sulk, cry, and fall apart. But after that, we need to pick ourselves up and move on.

We often lean on other people for support, which is justified and fundamentally how humans work and co-exist. However, we can not rely on someone to walk for us; the messy work is that of our own. This is because only after that does growth welcome us and enter our soul. If we depend on someone else to walk for us, we will always be depending on their availability. We will seek validation from them because they are the ones leading us. When we heal ourselves from within, we validate ourselves. This way, we don't allow anyone to come in and bombard their opinion on us. Brandon was blamed for Point Shaving, but he knew how honest he was in his heart. And so, what people said did not matter to him. Because his loss was his own, and his win was his pride.

If you let an injury stop you, it's on you. If you allow a mistake to stop you, that is another mistake you are welcoming in your life. If you think about it, there is nothing that can physically harm your potential. Your greatest potential is your will; everything else that comes next is secondary. When the roots are strong, the tree can survive any storm. However, if the roots are weak, the storm doesn't need to make an effort because the tree will manage to destroy itself independently.

As long as you believe that God is taking care of you, you feel less tense. This is because then you leave your affairs up to Him. Once you do that, you don't feel pressured to complete each and every task. God can move mountains, open locked doors, and create new pathways at any time. I shared Brandon's story because I believe we feed on evidence. We live on seeing something physically if we want to believe in the possibility of it existing. Brandon's is evidence. He is clear proof of God's work and how faith can raise you from the ashes so remarkably.

We are born in a world that thrives because of greed. The greed of not just attaining more money, but more power, belief, and achievement. This is why we often think we are born to lose. There is so much competition around us that we fail to believe in our own success and capacity.

Our greed is built on the success we have stolen from other people. People may look at you and destroy your plans before you embark on your journey. Multiple occurrences similar to this may shift your view regarding yourself. Everyone on this Earth has the chance to become successful, and that chance can only be exacerbated from within. We all are born with capabilities that can make us successful, whether we are born poor or rich. It really just becomes a matter of if we want to achieve that success. As much as success requires a belief in God, the main push comes from within. You need to believe in yourself and your potential. Let me ask you:

"Why do you think you cannot do it?"

God is fair and just. So do you think it's possible that he granted someone else everything and let you be with the bare minimum?

I came from the bare minimum. I was raised by a single mother and lived below the poverty line. Today, I am Kerry Carter. Sometimes, we let ourselves off the hook by making excuses for our situations and thus blaming other people. Sometimes, the underlying fault is ours, but we project it onto our circumstances. One of the mere facts of life which, as humans, is tough for us to accept, and justifiably so, is our fear from our own selves. Accepting ourselves as the barrier to our circumstances makes us fear in-depth research regarding who we are. It makes us vulnerable and exposes us to new discoveries.

We are also well aware that our circumstances may only change when we make a move to change them. By definition, circumstance means a situation connected with an event or a specific action; they are like variables. When it is tough to change the physical aspect of a situation, we must take control of our mental health then. When you strengthen yourself and your belief mentally, you allow yourself to be more patient and calmer.

Humans are born in all colors, all shapes, and sizes. Therefore, our physical features cannot be a space for judgments or biasness. For what is out of our control, we should not feel guilty nor responsible. We can, however, control what we can. All of our aspects may be interlinked, but if you dig deep enough, you will understand there is still so much that is under our control. People and our circumstances may take away everything from us, but no matter how hard they try, they will never be able to take away your growth, and that is your greatest strength.

Look within and seek to open doors that God has already unlocked for you. In order to help ourselves, we also need to be open to the idea of helping others. This is one of the most beautiful ways in which God works. He helps us discover ourselves as we help others – kill two birds with one stone. Helping others also plays a great role in our lives because we validate ourselves and make ourselves feel better about ourselves.

If I am not willing to help someone with the little that I have, how can I expect God to send help in return? Human beings are made for other human beings, and we are sent down to each other to help each other. For example, I was sent to Brandon by God. I provided Brandon with the resources he needed to succeed, and he helped me find perspective. Oh wow!

I just realized that's exactly what I said to myself in the mirror this morning. I'm not writing this book with the intention to preach, but more with the idea of spreading my experiences out there. Sometimes, we have all that we need and want, but what we lack is peace. We search for that peace internally and externally, but to no avail. We eventually realize that we're looking for it the wrong way. Sometimes, our answers are not within us, and they are within other people. Perhaps, that's why people are spontaneously placed in our lives many times, leaving us shocked at His ways.

God is our friend. He is a friend who has all the power. Befriending Him will make life easier because you'll develop a special bond with him. Our life is not meant to be a single journey. It is to influence and to be influenced by many others. For me, it is important that I have solid faith in something greater than myself, perhaps, some sort of Oneness. It helps me stay stable and hopeful. When I remind myself of the greater power, I do not just tell myself that someone's taking care of me; I also remind myself that I'm not alone. If I'm not alone, then why would anyone else be? That, however, is difficult to explain to people who may feel melancholic and gloomy. This is where you translate your energy to them and hold their hand as they walk and restore their energy.

This leads me to my next point. We are built to win. It is important for us first to understand who we are, what we want, and who we want to be. To succeed, we have to believe that God is looking after us. That way, we feel hopeful and look forward to the future. It helps us stay grounded and not lose track of who we are as well.

Our job is to work hard, and God's work lies in our results. He backs us up and looks after us in every step. Sometimes the delays that take place are to reroute us to a better location. Other delays are to make us more patient and resilient for what's to come. Brandon is living proof of God's kindness, and I am living proof of God's mercy. He is looking after us. But you know how it goes:

If you don't have faith in yourself, you won't succeed or reach the heights you want to grasp. If you have faith, you feel slightly more composed and in shape. This is because you've left matters beyond your control up to the one who does control them. This eases you down and when you sit and think:

Everything is smooth.

You now handle your part of the journey, and God shall handle his part. This way, everything is smooth sailing, and you don't feel alone as well. God works in mysterious ways, many of which we might never be able to understand. However, this does not mean that we cannot achieve or that we are blind to the realities of the world. We are not. We are simply more strategic and pragmatic.

You cannot go on living blindly and wait for the next big thing to surprise you. Always set a plan, whether it is short-term or long-term. You do you, and the rest is up to Him. He may delay it, but He will never disappoint, for He is all we really have. Brandon's success was mainly due to his hard work and self-belief, but his belief in God played a key role. Similarly, God played an integral role in my success, and I believe He is all you as well need to succeed.

CHAPTER 5:
SHANNON SHORTER

There are people God sends down to us as lessons, many of which pose as a reality check. We have to be careful with how we treat the people that enter our lives and the demeanor we use, considering everyone has their own battles to fight.

Many times, the people in our lives set themselves as examples of their character. They prove themselves through their kindness, strength, empathy, and will. One such person was Shannon Shorter. If you never knew who he was, well, now you do. Shannon was one of my youngest brothers, and I'm grateful to God for blessing me with his presence. Not just his presence, but exposing me to who he is and how he perceives life. I feel grateful for being a part of his success and for playing a role in the man he has become.

The one aspect about Shannon that is solid and unshakeable is his faith in God. It was almost as if Shannon could see God and how He worked. I remember watching Shannon strive to make it every day. The young lad worked out, read his Bible, and prayed regularly. He knew it was only God he could rely on. Shannon knew God had the highest power, and so he made the smart choice of directly conversing with the one who had the ability to grant it to us. Shannon had direction, and that helped him steer clear of changes that could potentially wreck him. Shannon remembered God by reciting the Bible every day. As he read the words of God, he reminded himself of his purpose. As Shannon prayed, he asked God for what he wanted. Shannon was a man of confidence. His faith didn't shake with one rocky road or a few extra hurdles.

Shannon was a walking testimony. If you figured the odds he beat in life, the hurdles he crossed single-handedly, and how he stood in the face of adversity with his head held high; your jaw would drop. Shannon's story is one of survival – survival of the fittest may have given upon. I remember Shannon entering my sports bar in hopes of working with me. However, he did not just dive into sports. Shannon started off by working the parking lots.

Shannon is proof that if you have a dream, then you have the potential to achieve it. You will never envision something that is beyond your understanding or capacity. This is why if you do have a dream, you need to find ways to protect it. The essence of a dream lies in it being far-fetched. It is a mode for us to believe in ourselves and all that we can be. Shannon had no issues working in the rain, sleet, snow, or heat. Shannon had a dream, and the boy knew there was no one to blame except himself if he didn't fulfill them.

Shannon's testimony is enough to encourage anyone to hold on to their dream because in times like these, when we feel we are alone, knowing that someone is around us can help us.

Shannon Shorter went from worrying about his next meal to earning six figures as he played basketball overseas. It can get tough, and you may be convinced that there's no hope in sight, but that does not mean that it won't get better. Your current situation does not define your future situation. However, what you choose to do with your current state may have an intense effect on how your future may unfold. If we don't gamble on ourselves, how can we expect anyone else to do it for us? There is no one who shall give us anything in this world, and we will always have to go out and earn it.

We need to take that leap of faith and place the trust in ourselves first before placing it in other people. After we seek confidence within ourselves, it is only then that we can give part of it to others. We cannot give empty pieces of ourselves to anyone because we will fail. Not only will we be giving away a part of ourselves, but we will also be doing great injustice to our own souls.

Put in the work, the days and the nights, and soar. This does not mean just engaging in physical labor but also mental work. In order to be successful, it is fundamental that you understand yourself and the layers you hide your reality within. When you embark on a journey to understanding who you are, you figure out your internal coping mechanisms and strategies. This will help you analyze the spectrum more clearly and in a much more transparent manner. Pragmatically speaking, you need to go out and earn what you desire to achieve. When I say earn, I genuinely mean earn it. The world will never hand us what we want, regardless of how many tantrums we may throw. This is why you go out, and you earn. Once you smell the whiff of your first paycheck, you'll feel some sort of attraction to it. Hence comes the good part. After you begin earning, you will find yourself carrying your own expenses and bills, and being independent is one of the most liberating feelings in the world.

For some of us, the road might be easier than others. Many roads might be smoother, while others might be rocky. This does not mean you give up without a fight. If there's a road, then there's a destination. Giving up always sounds tempting because it's convenient. You get to breathe and not worry about your focus anymore. But let me ask you:

"Where's the fun in that?"

We hold such high aspirations and visions, but we are almost always unaware of who we are and who we can be. The journey seems intense, and we always feel as if we can do well without it. However, that's where the real test lies. The real question lies in how much of a challenge you can welcome. Are you someone who takes life head-on and accepts, come what may? Or are you the type to sleep tight under the blanket? Pretending may sound easier than accepting reality for what it is, but it is not one to take you very far. Unfortunately, giving up consumes more than we calculate, and picking ourselves up every time can be taxing and mentally draining. This is avoidable.

We get so anxious by fearing the distance that we sometimes lose touch with the essence of what we're searching for. The idea that dreams are a distant reality sets us two steps back. However, that is simply our perception. Our perception does not have to be the reality or a trademark set in stone. Our perception is one part of an opinion, and opinions are highly subjective. If dreams were rather easy to achieve, say as easy as crossing the street, then where would the challenge be? It would be something many would reject before investigating the opportunities it may bring. Dreams are not a ball in the park or a toy to play with in the backyard. They require persistence, hard work, effort, time, and dedication. That is why those who run after their dreams are examples of those who may not have faith in themselves.

If you dig deep and look closely, many highly regarded people converted their dreams into a reality. These people were pushed back, shunned, and made to believe that their reality was the only thing that existed – dreams were false hopes to live by until we die. But they rejected this notion because they believed in who they were, and they achieved it — examples such as Oprah Winfrey, JK Rowling, Steve Jobs, and many others. There are countless examples in the sports world as well. The most active example you can think of is the writer of this book – Kerry Carter. When I was growing up as a child, I had every reason to believe that my dream was always just a dream. But I blatantly rejected that idea. When you put in effort honestly, and with integrity, you will be surprised to see how much the Universe can favor you. The only factor that can help you truly achieve your dream is your brain. What you think, how you think, and what you CHOOSE to welcome in your life play a role greater than you think. Achieving dreams is not easy, but here's a secret – your current situation can only be a hindrance on your way.

If you dream of being a basketball player, you should be the first person to enter the gym and the last one to exit it. You must work on your game every day regardless of the outcome. To become successful, you must strive for success daily. One major contributing factor for achieving your dream is also an aspect many fail at. This factor plays an integral role in how far you go and how much you can bear it. This factor is known as Commitment.

According to Google, Commitment is defined as some sort of an obligation. It is a duty that requires you to dedicate yourself to a certain something. To achieve your dream, you need to commit. In order to succeed, you will have to put in effort daily and consistently. You need to prove to your dreams that you can handle the responsibility that comes with them.

I say this to anyone who tells me they have a dream. When they ask me for advice, I often say,

"Achieving a goal is not everyone's cup of tea. There is a lot you have to give up to reach where you want to. Because the heights you want to reach are not available for everyone, sometimes, you have to let people go. We outgrow many people in our life, and that is because we are growing up and expanding. That's a good thing."

Sacrifice is another aspect that plays a vital role in how far you wish to travel. These journeys are often lonely because they can get intense and mentally taxing. However, a dream is a dream. This is why the rewards are immense and why the saying, "the grass is greener on the other side," is true. Life has its ups and downs, and we have to believe that no matter what life may throw at us, we can and will overcome it.

There's this thing in our lives which we often misinterpret. It is the difference between what life is and what the Universe is. Life is known as the existence of an individual or a mortal being. The Universe includes space, energy, the movement of time and fundamentally encapsulates all that surrounds us. It is not limited to what humans are and what they do. Perhaps, that is the beauty of the war we humans have with ourselves. The Universe is our saving grace. It protects us from other people and, most importantly, from ourselves. Life may throw a curveball at you, but that is when the Universe will enter and save you, without you knowing. Sometimes we achieve our dreams, and sometimes we don't. This does not mean you don't get to give it a shot.

Renowned Chef Gordon Ramsay once had a dream of becoming a professional football player. He was getting close and closer until one day, and he found himself hurting his knee. Like anyone else would have thought, Ramsay, considered it to be a normal injury. Until one day, his doctors informed him that his knee injury may not allow him to become a football player, ever. This shattered Ramsay. He then diverted towards cooking, and as of 2020, Gordon Ramsay has 16 Michelin Stars to gloat. The Universe will continue to look after you long after you have given up. What it requires from us is simply placing our faith and honesty in it.

Overnight success is dishonest. It is not faithful and will fall at the same rate it rose at. The passion with which overnight success occurs is questionable. It questions the very idea of where the essence of achievement lies. You will meet people who will lie to you and say they can help, simply extracting money from you. 95% of the people you meet will ask you for money and say that's all you need to get to the top. That is not completely true. I did not have money, yet I made it to the top. The 95% may disguise themselves to fool you, but be mindful that there exists another 5% too. These 5% naturally attract wholesome, authentic, and genuine energy.

I have, so far, provided examples of four young men, all from very different backgrounds. I couldn't help but notice all of them had one aspect in common – their faith in God. All four of them are well off now as professional athletes in their won sport. All four of them faced some sort of adversity, but they overcame them all. I'd like to think it's all part of God's plan. You need not worry about what other people will think or say because they will continue to do it even after you're successful. These people tend to feed on your insecurities and use that strategy to prevent your success.

Shannon's story is one of resilience, strength, trials, but more importantly, strength. Shannon is an exemplary embodiment of what it means to be strong in the face of adversity and to digest pride when you have reached the ranks of superiority because you have lived on the other side. His story is one of being humble and embracing reality instead of rejecting it. Once you embrace reality, you start working on what's truly important, and that's what Shannon did – he worked on himself.

CHAPTER 6:
JONATHAN SIMMONS

The next example is a true force of respect. He is one of God's gifts to the world – Jonathan Simmons. God allowed me to be a part of his life, and for that, I am grateful. I witnessed Jonathan's work first hand, and I feel as if it was in return for any empathy I may have shown at any point in time, or any good I may have been a part of, in my life.

You will come across many people in your life, some will make you re-consider your values, and some will teach you the meaning of life subconsciously. Our desires in this world are many, but our approach is what determines what happens to that desire – how far we go and how far we don't.

It's all about my younger brother. This chapter is all about him, and perhaps, the next one too. I say this because Jonathan did not sit down to fix the broken; he took his broken pieces and created something exemplary. The man he became is not the man he would have become had he had received all of life's blessings. The struggles life placed in his life built him into a credible man with values and morals that could not be compromised on.

The journey began in 2012 when I received a call from my friend, Dwayne Rodgers, aka *THE LEDGEN*. Dwayne is the best street ballplayer to ever come out of Houston, Texas, who has touched a basketball.

I remember Dwanye called me on a Friday to ask if I was going to the gym on Sunday.

"Hey, did I disturb you?"

"Hey! Oh, no-no. You didn't. What's up? You good?"

"I just wanted to ask if you were going to go to the gym on Sunday."

"Yeah, I will."

"Cool. I have someone I want to introduce you to."

"Who?"

"You'll see."

Our conversation ended, and I went about my life. The nature of our careers was such that we would introduce our acquaintances to people we knew. That Sunday, at around 3 pm, I walked into the Forge gym to get my team 'Houston Live' ready to play. As I was prepping up, Dwayne walked up to me alongside a kid who knew he was ready to play.

The kid looked like he knew what he wanted. His walk was assertive yet calm. His aura was fierce yet composed. Dwayne knew who he was introducing me to, but as I looked at the kid, I felt as if I already knew him – for he was a vision of my past. The boy who just walked up to me knew his future before it even took flight, and that's what drove me towards him. He knew life wasn't sparkles and unicorns. If he wanted half the sparkles in his view, he knew he would have to work twice as hard.

Dwayne introduced me to Jonathan Simmons and told me all the kids needed to soar the right kind of help to back him up. The very first day I met Jonathan, Dwayne told me about Jonathan's potential. Dwayne had only good words to remember Jonathan by, and as much as those words provided me validation, what gave me even more validation was simply witnessing Jonathan's energy. I told Jonathan to come back next weekend, and we'll play at 4 pm, and frankly, I'd let him play because I wanted to see how he was. I wanted to witness him play on my own despite what I thought of him when I saw him.

The following Sunday, I went inside the gym only to see he was already there standing and talking to a group of men. I walked over to him and handed him a uniform. As I was getting my team ready to play, I noticed the gym began filling up with spectators who watched us play. Dwayne walked over to me and said,

"Watch this, homeboy. You'll love the way he plays."

From the moment the ball was thrown at the players to the last second until the game ended, Jonathan put up a show. He was phenomenal and exemplary. Jonathan's energy, his flow, his aura, and his authenticity shone bright and high throughout the entire game. The boy did not drain out for a single second. It was as if basketball was all he wanted to play, tirelessly. We won the game, and Jonathan played like a superstar. He was wonderful and impeccable. The relationship he held with the ball was one to be understood. It could not be deciphered by the normal man – it needed someone with passion and resilience.

I told Jonathan to call me later that night, and he said that he would. At around 8 pm, my phone rang, and as I picked up my phone to accept the call, I saw it was Simms who called me. I told him I was going to go to the Fonde Gym at 11 am in morning, and he said he'd be there. As I walked into the gym at around 11.15 am, I noticed Simms was playing on the court. I watched him win four games in a row. The fifth game was the one he lost. After he lost his game, Simms walked over to me and shook my hand, and we sat down and began to talk. Simms told me he wanted to play basketball professionally and make it to the NBA.

"I want to get into the NBA, basically."

"You know all you need to do for that is simply go for it? Don't give up on your dream, kid. It's only yours to have."

"I've gotten into trouble in the past, and because of my actions, I was on probation for a while."

"Oh!"

"Yeah, but there's another problem. Besides probation being on my record, I'm also slightly behind on my probation fees. I'm not working as well, so that's kind of a problem."

"If you decide not to quit and not give up, I'll stand behind you. If you, however, do intend to back out, I won't be able to do much. All I need from you is the will to continue moving forward. And with regards to your probation fees, let me take care of it."

"Big bro, if you do this for me, if I make it, you make it," Jonathan said as he looked up to me, with eyes full of hope.

As I looked back at him, I said

"Not 'if,' but 'when!'"

I reached into my pocket and handed Simms $200 so that he could pay his probation fees and keep some money for himself. I left the gym soon after and went to my Sports Bar in Houston Live downtown, which was just across the street from Minute Maid Park.

Later, I phoned Jonathan and told him if he wanted to earn extra money, he could come and work in the parking lot doing events at Minute Maid Park. Jonathan was ever-ready and said he would come right then.

Even though this happened years ago, I remember watching Simms, Shannon, and T Hoop parking cars in my parking lot right under the sun, which scorching heat attacking their skins. To the boys, it didn't matter if the sun was out was if thunderstorms were moving mountains. What mattered was that work was getting done. As time passed, I reached out to different contacts in order to find Simms an opportunity to play basketball and help him earn some money that would help him support his family.

A few days later, I received a phone call from Darrel, who was out of California. He told him he had a Clint in Houston that was starting a new team in Sugar Land and needed help in putting a team and an organization together. I told Darrel that I was willing to help him set it up.

Darrel had given my contact to a few ladies. I received a call from them at around 11 am, on a Wednesday morning.

"Hi, is this Kerry Carter?"

"Yes, this is Kerry. I'm sorry, who is this?"

"We're Tamara and Arnetta. Darrel gave us your number. Is this a good time?"

"Yes, of course. Although I do want to know, am I speaking with Tamara or Arnetta?"

"This is Tamara, Arnetta's sitting with me."

"Oh, okay."

"Alright. So Darrel referred you and told us you could help set up our team and organization."

"Yes, I'm very connected, and I have a widespread reach."

"Would you help us?"

"Yes."

"Hi, Kerry. Arnetta here. Could you come and sit with us? I feel like a face-to-face meeting would be more ideal. We would be better able to go over what we want to do."

"Sure, when?"

"Around 1-2 o'clock."

I arrived at Arnetta's house at 1.30 pm. I knocked on the door, and seconds later, I watched her open the door and welcome me inside. Tamara and Arnetta and told me they primarily needed a coach who would attract attention, and at that moment, just the right person I needed to call – my good friend, Hall of Fame Calvin Murphy.

"Kerry, can you really get him to coach our team?"

"Tamara, I think yes. I'll call him and see."

As I was leaving, I called Calvin, and he told me he was at Church. Nonetheless, Calvin asked me to come over to the Church and tell him what I had in mind.

I drove over to the Southwest Baptist Church to meet with Calvin and told him whatever was happening. I told him Tamara and Arnetta needed someone to coach, and more importantly, someone who would get attention to increase popularity. Calvin looked at me and said,

"My brother, I am very much interested in coaching the team."

I was ecstatic.

I gave Arnetta's number to Calvin and told him to call her directly and speak to her regarding any questions he may have. This coaching job may be a great opportunity for him, but he deserved to see if the job deserved him too.

After Calvin spoke to the ladies, Tamara and Arnetta gave him the coaching job on the spot. Calvin called me then and told me he was good to go. He liked the job, and the women also saw him as a good fit. Calvin said something to them that got my blood pumping, and it was after a while that I felt this elevated. He said,

"Let's start getting those players together, my friend!"

"I already have three boys on standby for you. Jonathan Simms, BJ, and T Hooper are all ready for the show to begin."

After going over the rules, Simms figured he would first have to be drafted in order to receive a top contract from the team, and so we sent Jonathan to San Antonio to participate in the pre-draft tryouts.

Personally, I felt relieved that Jonathan had a ray of hope to look forward to. I knew he would end up somewhere good, and one day, make it to the NBA too. However, I wanted to make sure it happened quickly. The boy relied on me, and more than that, he was an honest lad. This opportunity was the perfect way for him to climb up the ladder.

I have come across many young boys with a dream, and I've wanted to help each one of them. This is because I know the struggle, I know the divide, I know the uncertainty, and I know the disagreements our minds have with our hearts. Jonathan Simmons taught me you could change the course of your life with just determination. If you consistently tell your brain that you will make it, at one point, your brain will agree with you. This is due to many reasons. Our heart has too much power. This is because of how much energy and passion it creates. Our minds are our voice of reason, but many times, our determination rises higher than reason – and that's why the fire in us needs to stay alive.

CHAPTER 7:
THE SMELL OF HARD WORK

We told Jonathan not to go and show up in the games or the drills because then nobody else would be able to draft him. Our plan worked just as we thought it would. We received the number 3 pick of the first-round picks, and Simms was our pick. Jonathan was able to receive the top contract because he was the first-round draft pick. His contract was for $1800 a month. Jonathan was also provided with a free room and a board at the Sugar Land Marriott. From there, the Sugar Land Ledgens was formed, and Jonathan eventually became the star player to lead them to the first-place spot in the league.

In his first game, Simms scored 66 points as if it was a walk in the park. The season ended shortly before it was intended to, which is why we never got the chance to play for the championship. While all of this was happening, I was reaching out to my contacts in an attempt to try to get Simmons a big contract to play somewhere better than the ABL League. As time passed, I started receiving phone calls for Simms to play overseas for $5000-$10-000 a month.

In his first game, Simms got 66 points as if it was a walk in the park. I told Jonathan about it, ad he told me that he had to get his passport to play. I did tell Jonathan that we should go for it. He then told me that he would have to get off of his probation first.

"I need to get done with my probation first, you know."

"We'll work on it."

This is where the devil came in. In an attempt to destroy the young boy's dream. Jonathan visited his probation officer to ask how much he had to pay off to rid himself off of his fines and restitution completely.

Jonathan was told that he still had to pay the remaining $16,000.00, and he had no choice but to get a lawyer to advise him before he stood in front of the judge. It was important for Jonathan to go to the judge because he would then release him. After Simmons left his probation officer's office, Simmons called me.

"They're asking me to pay $16,000. I'll also need a lawyer who can help me establish my case in front of the judge."

"We'll do something, don't worry."

I didn't have that kind of money, and especially since it was needed all at once. However, I did have some money that I needed to put up for my property Taxes. Hence, I walked out on faith and didn't pay my taxes. I gave Jonathan my tax money and asked him to follow his dream. I was holding on to hope just as Jonathan was holding on to me.

After I took the money out of the bank and handed them to Simms, on the next probation visit, we went to Sack and Save and purchased money orders to pay off Joantahn's probation fines and restitution. From there, I hired a lawyer for $15,000.00 to take his case back to court in front of the judge to get him an early release off of probation.

After we went to court prepared, we asked the judge for an early release. We were naïve. Naïve enough to not understand the devil's work and interference. But the devil is also always naïve. More than naïve, the devil is unaware – unaware of God's power.

The judge denied him an early release and also told him there was no way she was going to let him off early. The judge was stern and assertive. I had my lawyer go back to her twice but to no avail. She said no both times; however, the next time my lawyer visited her, she said if Jonathan complied with everything for 30 days, she would let him go. That was good news, all on its own.

Jonathan felt those 30 days pass by as slowly as it was possible. But, I did not lose faith. Neither did Jonathan. The boy just needed space to breathe. He had been exhausted for a while now, and the entire process was overwhelming for him. It became an even more crucial time for him because he wanted to go for the pre-draft tryouts, but his probation came in between.

However, 30 days eventually passed by, and Jonathan and I were simply holding onto the ray of light the judge handed us. Little did we know, the devil never gives up. After 30 days, the judge said no. This goes to show that people who reside at higher places and authority can also hinder your pat. I knew I had to hold on to my faith at that point. We had come so far, and I was not going to let Jonathan fall back now, especially now.

Jonathan walked out of the courtroom crying, and I could see the pain in his eyes. The young boy was helpless. He just wanted to play. He wasn't asking for much, but he was asking for a less traumatic path. Jonathan was crying, and he was highly disappointed. I walked up to my little brother and told him to hold his head high and that God has a plan for us – I knew it in my heart.

A week later, Jonathan called me and told me that he was going to try out for the Austin Toros in Austin, Texas, the D League for the San Antonio Spurs.

Jonathan told me he needed money and a ride to Austin. I told Simms to go for it, and I handed him $250 and a key to my black S550. He left and went to Austin. Three days later, I sat down and wondered if Simms was doing okay since I hadn't heard from him. At around 11.30 am that Wednesday morning, Simms called me and said,

"Big bro, I made the team."

"You bet I told you, you were going to make it!"

"But I won't be able to come back right now. I need to stay here until Friday with your car, though."

"Oh, don't worry about that, kid. I drive my truck around; that's alright."

"Thanks, man."

Friday arrived, and Simms drove up to my house and I, then drove him to his mother's house and dropped him off there. That Saturday night, I received a phone call from Simms.

"Hey, big bro."

"Yes, my boy?"

"I'm going to have to ask for a favor."

"Anything."

"I need you to bring the truck to pick me up because I need to load my things up and take them to Austin with me."

"No problem, I got it for you."

I never said no to Simms. I was always there for the boy whenever he needed me, and that's fundamentally how one should stand behind someone. I picked Jonathan up along with his things and drove him to Austin, Texas, to drop him off. After we unloaded my truck, Jonathan looked at me and said,

"Big bro, you got a few dollars?"

I reached my hand out to my pocket and gave him $175. He asked me to take him to Walmart so that he could get something to eat and buy himself a shower curtain. We hopped on to Walmart, and Jonathan bought all that he needed. I then dropped him off at his new place in Austin and drove to Houston.

Jonathan was still on probation and was out of Harris County. To make matters worse, he had left the state of Texas without his probation officer's permission to do so. Everything went fine in the first year in the D League, but in his last year, the devil stepped in and tried to destroy everything that God had put together for Jonathan. Priority Sports Simms agent had gotten a spot in the NBA Summer League where Simms would play in Orlando.

At that point in time, I was in Chicago with my team HOUSTON Live playing in the TBT and Nike Pro-Am. While in Chicago, I received a call from Reggie congratulating me since we were now part of the San Antonio Spurs roster. Simms was picked up by the Spurs for two years.

I hung up the phone with Reggie, and 20 minutes later, my phone rang. It was Jonathan. He called me and was crying on the phone as he said,

"It's over, big bro. We made it."

"Remember I told you, God has a plan."

Later on, the Spurs flew Simms to Las Vegas, where he would go on to win the NBA Summer League Championship and the Championship MVP. Simms put on a show that summer that sent shockwaves across the NBA and the world. After returning home to Houston, Simms probation officer and the judge had gotten a word of him being out of the states and out of Harris County.

The judge then put out a warrant for Jonathan's arrest. Jonathan went to report to his probation officer and was arrested on the spot. When this was happening, I was at home with my family when I received a phone call from Jonathan.

"Big bro, it's over. They're taking me to jail."

I was in disbelief, unsure of what was going on. I could hear it in Jonathan's voice. He was in fear of losing his opportunity – the one he had just gotten. He didn't even get the chance to relive it fully.

"Don't worry. It's all going to take care of itself. We are in God's hands." I comforted Simms.

I hung up the phone and called Reggie. Reggie told me not to worry and that they would have him out of there in a little while.

When I tell you God will test your faith over and over again, I give you the perfect example.

The next morning, Simmons called me saying he was out on bond and that they hired a lawyer to take care of everything. He also told me he was no longer on probation and that burden was lifted off of him. He was a free man now. When he told me this, I looked up to the sky and stared at it, in awe of his power and mercy.

It goes to show you that if we don't see God's work, it does not mean he's not working. Simms is now going in his 3rd year in the NBA, two years with Spurs, and his new home with the Orlando Magic. Jonathan is the true meaning of a second chance. We are all born to lose, and we are all built to win.

CHAPTER 8:
FAITH

Faith can never be forced onto anyone. It is independent in nature and divine in its form. Anyone's faith does not depend on another human being. It is different from seeking validation. It is fundamentally relying on a sole power. Faith is beyond human understanding, which is why it helps us remain grounded and calm in the face of hopelessness and absolute fright.

Faith can be in anything; it can exist in our talent, relying upon our strength, believing in another human being, or depending on a power that exceeds the heavens and the Earth. In times of darkness, it can be tough to rely on a power that we can not see. However, that is the essence of faith – believing in the existence of God and His power to help us get out of a problem without ever seeing him. When you develop faith, you realize you never need to see God because you will always feel Him within you. God does not reside up above only. He lives within us, which is why we feel so close to Him, despite never being able to see Him. *This is what faith is.*

Faith can help us hold on to the idea of a silver lining, which in turn moves us away from the idea of ending our lives or harming ourselves. This is because we leave our decisions up to a higher power, with the trust that someone greater is looking after us. Faith allows us to breathe and take a break. *This is how faith helps us exist.*

Faith plays a huge role in helping us believe in our dreams. We dream big, and many of our dreams have prerequisites that we can not afford. Yet, we believe that God will find a way for us. And so, He always does. He does not disregard our plans; he only delays them. That, too, is for our own benefit. The delay is fundamentally a process that prepares us to accept our dreams when they come to us. For example, the twins I spoke about at the start of my book. Jamal and Jamel were two young boys with a dream. They could not become the men they wanted to become at that age. Life is a process, and nature will always play its course, with attempts made to test our loyalty, determination, and thirst. The boys held on to faith as they continued to work hard. They did not know how they'd make it, but what they did know was that they wanted to. And so they did. *This was Jamal and Jamel's faith.*

Through the stories in the book, there are lessons as to why people held on to hope and why faith played an integral role in their success. They could have just as easily given up. It was all a matter of wanting it or believing they couldn't get there. One of the reasons all of these boys were successful in achieving their dreams was that they knew they wanted it. They completed their part of the job with diligence and patience. When it was time for God to shine, they calmly watched.

We often confuse our current situation with the future we aspire to have. What we don't realize is that our present conditions do not depict our future, which is why we are in the present. Our present exists so that we work for our future. This, mixed with God's plan, is what our future is. In your present, you cannot witness your future, or else the sweet taste of victory won't taste the same.

When we dream, we take a leap of faith. We place our trust in God, but we also place our trust in ourselves and our ability to reach the skies we see every day. We might win; we might lose. But at least we would have tried. You cannot assume what your future will be based on what your present is now. Our judgment is as limited as it gets. Work on what you want, and you will find yourself at your desired destination before you know it. The process of reaching our destination is one where we have to give it our all, for example, Jonathan Simmons. Although Simmons had paid off his probation debt, he was still denied freedom. The judge used their power, but they could not compete with God's power. Simmons landed a spot in the NBA Summer League. He made it there because of his honesty towards his profession and his hunger to make it through. The rest was God's work.

Life is not an easy-going journey. It is supposed to be tumultuous, and it is bound to make us fall to the ground. You may hit rock-bottom many times in life, and you may never see a silver lining. But you will somehow end up fighting for dear life. The famous quote goes as follows:

"You want to die? Then throw yourself into the sea, and you'll see yourself fighting to survive. You do not want to kill yourself, and rather you want to kill something inside of you."

We grow tired of our troubles but are unaware of how to separate ourselves from our pain. This leads to hopelessness, grief, and a loss of faith in ourselves. Apart from faith in God, what is most important is to have faith in our own selves. All the boys that came to me and made it big had much in common, including determination and dedication. One of the factors that contributed to their success and helped them stay motivated towards their goal was the belief that they knew what they wanted. They had every reason to give up on their dream, but they chose to dream still.

The boys had faith in their game, they had faith in who they were, and more importantly, their love for basketball was honest, true, and powerful. They had every hurdle obstruct their way. At some points, extra problems came their way, ones that were never in the picture. But they knew nothing surpluses the love they had for basketball.

The pain everyone from Jamal and Jamel to Brandon Johnson to Shannon Shorter to Jonathan Simmons was so incredibly high, the boys had every reason to believe that fate wasn't playing along with their plan. But what the boys knew was that they never needed the validation of fate. For it was God who administered it.

God has a way of allowing people in our lives and removing them from our lives. I was born to a single mother who had to work multiple jobs to provide food on the table simply. I ended up becoming God's source. It is God's blessing upon me that I was a source of help for so many. I have always met people from different sources, and these links are beyond human understanding. But God made them happen. And he made them successful. I owe it to God. I was always just a source. I was one of them – someone with a dream. All I did was work hard and place my faith in God. I would sleep at night assured that someone was looking over me, looking over my plans, and protecting me.

Finding peace in the existence of God can help because then we don't feel alone in times of distress. We place our problems in God's hands and ask Him to take care of them for us, for we know the beauty of God. One of the reasons we feel light and taken care of when we have faith in God is because we don't just place our faith in Him; we also believe in all he can give us, besides the fulfillment of our dreams. We believe in his mercy, his kindness, his shelter, and the fact that he knows us more than we will ever know ourselves. It is comforting to know that someone of power knows us better than we know ourselves, and that helps greatly when passively negative thoughts begin to intrude and convince us to think otherwise.

Faith makes us slightly stronger. Because then we don't feel lost. We do not feel as if nothing is out of shape or out of place. We sleep comfortably and securely. *Perhaps, that's the purpose of faith – to provide security in a place where we are constantly made to feel insecure.*

Life is about consistently making jumps. You're bound to land somewhere. If not the moon, then you'll find yourself amongst the stars. If you don't find yourself with stars, then maybe that specific jump was destined for the experience, for you to see the world without any commitments – as if a free visit. The next jump may require practical implementation of what you witnessed in the last jump.

The most important thing to do is to have a dream. Don't let anyone else take away your dream. For when you begin to dream of something, you don't have to pay for it at that point in time. You also don't have to justify it. You are also not required to let anyone know unless you desire to. Your dream is the most non-dramatic asset you have, and it is just yours. You don't even need to share it with someone. Something that is solely yours and will continue to remain yours. Then why should you give it up? If you have faith in your plans and where you want to be, and you have faith that God will take you there, then why not embark on a journey that has the potential to help you soar the sky independently. Who knows, you may land in the heavens?

CHAPTER 9:
PAST EXPOSURE

My life has not been roses and basketball successions since the start. My mom did work multiple jobs to provide for me, but she also had a lot to go through. Because she was occupied in simply making sure we had the next meal, there was much that went unattended. Life always took a turn for the worst; perhaps that's why I always relied on God. I knew I could not rely on anyone else, really. Ever since I was born, I faced heavy gruesome experiences, and many times, I was incredibly powerless. At this point in time, I am powerful enough to stand up for myself and reject any misbehavior or disrespect projected towards me.

However, when I was young, I did not have the power or the understanding. I was helpless and dependent. I can't blame my mother. As much as I should have been protected, my mother's hands were tied too. It was simply nature's way of teaching me so much and evolving me into the person I've become. I was only three years old when I was abused by my mother's boyfriend. Not only that, but he also attempted to kill me, but with God's grace, I made it out. How can three-year-olds protect themselves from such intimate torture? This is why I believe God is always looking after me; I made it out of that situation at a time when I had no sense of right or wrong, harmful or harmless, and was unaware of any measures to protect myself. This is why I believe I can always get out of a situation that may project me as helpless. Over time, I realized it is us who are helpless, and God is never helpless. And so, it is never a problem for him to extract us out of a difficult situation – we just have to ask him to help us do that.

I was then placed in foster care and stayed there for three years until I was six years old. At the age of six, I was returned to my mother, and that somehow made me stronger. Not sure why, probably because I was returned back to my mother, and the rush of blood and familiarity played a role.

My dynamic with my mother was rather complicated. Although it never affected me because I never knew how to love her or share love like a mother and son would, on a normal basis. I did not experience unconditional love, but it didn't bother me because I couldn't grieve a love I had never experienced. I never knew who my father was, and even now, after so many years, I am unaware of his existence. My mom never told me, and so, I never asked.

In the course of our lives, we come across people who consistently put us down. They place us in a position that restricts us from showing our true selves or from engaging and socializing. These people often come in the shape of close friends or family. They deliberately near themselves in an attempt to reach a place where they hold power. Once they are successful, they take full advantage of their position and importance to invalidate us or bring us down, especially if we are vulnerable.

Our vulnerability is our greatest asset which is also why it is a potential weakness. It guards us strongly, but it is also the same weapon used to bring our walls down. I have been a vulnerable young lad for the most part of my life, but I could never be taken advantage of because I had lived a rough life before.

I was not protected or sheltered. As sad as that may sound, it did prepare me for a tougher life. This is probably why I never took everything to heart and was also cautious of what was being said and told to me. I survived the street life early on, and so I was wary of what I was being told. Also, if I'm being honest, no one ever really brought me down. I feel as if God compensated for the life I had before. I never looked back at the past because I had so much to be grateful for as of now.

Also, I have always been people-friendly, so if anything, they were always rather helpful.

I was introduced to basketball by WES Crockett and Al Haymon, and ever since then, I knew it was the one for me. Basketball provided me with a sort of comfort I could not find anywhere else, and it was a form of solace for me.

WES Crockett introduced me to the world of Sports and Entertainment with West World Entertainment.If I have to mention the name of someone who has helped me reach the heights I did, then it would be WES Crockett.

I do wish life treated me better. I am eternally grateful for the life I have right now but to think about the past is traumatizing. Such trauma you don't heal from in a day or two. I may have a good life right now, but I have a past. One I carry with me continuously. The positivity I have infused in myself has emerged from my endurance. So I would not want to take away my experiences. This means my past is attached to me. What I made out of it is solely on my record, but I do have one naïve wish: for it all to have been easier.

The abuse, wondering if we would have a roof over our heads, thinking about where we would get our next meal from, really kept us on our toes. We did not have much to go by, and it kept us alert. We were always on alert regarding ourselves, and that shifted my entire personality. I had to work my way around my personality because of this. So much and trauma and hurt could have been avoided if I had just one thing going on. But that's alright. I don't have any complaints. I reached an esteemed place out of nothing. Perhaps, it was God's way of showing that He gives, but at a time he feels is right.

I always did know that God was on my side because then I wouldn't have made it this far. It was his kindness and mercy that got me this far, and I will always be grateful to him for all that He has blessed me with.

I don't think I would want to change my life and my past. The man I am today is fundamental because of the experiences I endured in the past. Letting them go would mean letting go of all of my learning as well, and I don't think I would have learned better anywhere else. However, it wasn't easy going through all that I did. At first, I was very happy that I was going back to live with my mother after I spent a considerable amount of time with my fosterer. It was a dream come true. However, over the years, as I got older, I began to feel as if she was very selfish with her role as my mother.

I don't hold it against her, primarily because I can't hold it against her. I am thankful for all that she did to provide for me over the years. She did what she thought was best for me at the time. I don't carry any resentment towards her, simply facts. My childhood was what it was because much was taken away from me, which is fundamentally why I am always up to helping people reach their dreams because I know what it takes, or more accurately, to encourage someone or help to support them.

In some ways, I did take extra care of making sure my kids did not have to go through what I did. It is rather upsetting to wonder where your next meal will come from and how one would go about their day. Our lives are intertwined with each other's lives, so what we do, the decisions we make, and the journeys we embark on, have an effect on the people who surround us, adverse or not. I now make sure my kids do not just have the most basic necessities but also leisure that they can survive on, on days that are tough. For my children, it is important to know that their parents are looking out for them in ways they don't know, and more importantly, in ways they do know.

It is important for children to know that their parents are looking out for them, so they feel secure and safe. We need to take special care of our children and provide them with what they need. You should be stable enough first before you plan on starting a family. It is not the child's job to wonder how they will survive. And the parent should make sure the child does not go through that. We are accountable to our children, and more importantly, accountable to ourselves we give to our children. Their childhood is something they carry with themselves for a long time, and as much as I've grown, a part of me does wish my childhood was slightly less anxious.

Now that I have so much, I feel as if my ideal life would have included an honest childhood. You've read all that I went through in life, and by the grace of God, the ultimate power brought me through it. People want God to bring them out of storms, but you have to go through one in order for him to bring you out of the other. While that is true, I feel like a decent childhood would not have ruined much. I agree my experiences helped me greatly, but a little less trouble would have felt nice in an alternate universe.

Made in the USA
Middletown, DE
24 March 2023

27539274R00042